Summary of

# Essentialism

by Greg McKeown

**Instaread**

# Overview

Essentialism: *The Disciplined Pursuit of Less* is a self-help book by Greg McKeown. The book outlines a minimalist approach to tasks and obligations by focusing on truly important goals and learning to turn down opportunities that do not directly contribute to meeting those goals. The modern fixation with multitasking and having it all has paradoxically resulted in accomplished, motivated people doing many relatively unimportant things poorly while neglecting their true goals because they are afraid of refusing any request.

An Essentialist understands that they have many choices and that not making them is really making a choice for the status quo. They develop the ability to discern the important from the unimportant and completely ignore the unimportant. The Essentialist also understands that, sometimes, changing focus to something important requires a trade-off in regards to other things they sort of wanted.

The process of refocusing on the essential goals begins with exploring and evaluating whether the current tasks contribute to those goals. Essentialists seek their personal highest points of contribution. Then, the Essentialist eliminates anything nonessential and learns to turn down requests. The goal that drives them must be clear enough to define when it is accomplished. Finally, they must outline the schedule and steps that ensure the most important things are addressed regularly.

Leaders can particularly make use of essentialist principles by identifying a clear focus and clearly defined roles for team members, checking in often to remove obstacles, communicate with precision, and choosing only the best team members.

# Important People

Greg McKeown: Greg McKeown is the founder and CEO of a leadership and strategy design agency, THIS, Inc. He was inducted into the World Economic Forum's Forum of Young Global Leaders in 2012.

Dieter Rams: Dieter Rams is a consumer product designer for Braun who is associated with Functionalist design. He coined the "less but better" phrase used throughout Essentialism.

Erin Callan: Erin Callan was CFO of Lehman Brothers for six months, starting in 2008. She has since written about her work-life balance and given advice to other working women about priority setting.

Anna McKeown: Anna McKeown is the wife of Greg McKeown. She is a central character in many of Greg's anecdotes about family as a priority.

Jack Dorsey: Jack Dorsey co-founded Twitter and is the current CEO and founder of mobile payment company Square.

# Key Takeaways

1. Nonessentialism dominates work lives today while true priorities do not get needed attention. The thin distribution of effort results in poor quality work.

2. Essentialism is an approach that emphasizes finding a true, limited set of goals, defining them clearly, setting everything else aside, and not taking on additional responsibilities.

3. When someone refuses to prioritize or make decisions about what to take on versus what to refuse, other people will end up making the decision based on what they find important.

4. Discerning what is important requires understanding that less can be better. An easy way to decide what is important enough is to immediately rule out anything that is not obviously vital to the primary goal.

5. Focusing on the important few priorities can require an individual or organization to abandon other goals that are not vital but would be nice to have, which preserves resources and energy for the essential tasks.

6. Keeping the mind sharp and focused can be facilitated by intentionally isolating from distractions.

7. Learning to refuse opportunities can be challenging if someone is worried about the ramifications of that refusal. They can offer to consider it after something else is accomplished or ask the requester to decide what to de-prioritize.

8. An individual or organization should be able to define the key goal clearly enough to know when it has been accomplished and to know how much needs to be done to reach it.

9. Editing the nonessential out of all aspects of life allows the essential to become clear. Other strategies for placing emphasis on the essential include setting boundaries on when to be available for work and learning to let go of losses in other projects.

10. When finding ways to eliminate the nonessential from a process, focus on creating buffers for time and resources to avoid a rush, eliminating bottlenecks rather than creating additional processes, and structuring the process as a series of small steps.

11. Implementing essentialism in everyday life requires that essentialism be at the center of every decision made, rather than being applied only to certain decisions.

12. Leaders have the ability to enforce essentialism in their teams by choosing only the best members, clearly defining a limited range of goals and roles, optimizing communication, and following up often.

# Analysis

## Key Takeaway 1

**Nonessentialism dominates work lives today while true priorities do not get needed attention. The thin distribution of effort results in poor quality work.**

## Analysis

Successful people undergo four steps on their way to being overburdened when they approach things as Nonessentialists. First they succeed at their endeavors. Then they gain a reputation for dependability, and get more opportunities. They have fewer resources and less energy to devote to each new opportunity. Finally, they stray from their original successful approaches and end up contributing little to new projects. A Nonessentialist person or organization makes a little progress in many directions, rather than making significant progress toward the most important objective.

This should sound familiar to anyone who works in a corporation today, where multitasking and productivity have become the primary measure of an employee's worth. Many people assume that they can successfully tackle more than one duty at the same time while doing both competently but, even when doing two things as simple as talking on the phone and checking email, it is likely that an important email will accidentally be deleted or the conversation will go silent because the multitasker was not listening. Humans are only capable of performing one task at a time unlike computers with dual processors that perform several tasks at a time. Humans do not have two brains or the capacity to work at super speeds. Therefore, giving adequate focus to two tasks can only happen if one is an automatic habit. Even though this seems like common sense, convincing an organization to encourage employees to focus their attention and pare down their to-do lists would be difficult because the organization's attention is divided. Businesses particularly often have many different types of operations, obligations to customers as well as shareholders, and emphasis on both quality and quantity, all of which divide their resources and efforts.

# Key Takeaway 2

**Essentialism is an approach that emphasizes finding a true, limited set of goals, defining them clearly, setting everything else aside, and not taking on additional responsibilities.**

## Analysis

Essentialists have very few priorities on their list and those priorities are the ones closest to their heart. They are comfortable turning down any opportunity that does not make progress toward those goals. As a result, the Essentialist devotes as much attention to each priority as it deserves, not just as much as can be spared, so that nothing is too rushed or neglected.

Compared to the standard operating procedure of most people in business, the Essentialist approach might sound luxurious and impractical. On first glance, being an Essentialist would seem nice since there are so many people who claim to have too many obligations, but having only a couple goals while abandoning other, short-term projects at the same time might imply decreased productivity. However, this intense focus can be a powerful productivity booster when many people adopt it. If, while working on an annual report, the writers had nothing else on their schedules and all clearly understood their roles, the report would be completed much more quickly, and would probably be better written, than if the writers also had to juggle the press releases, proofreading, and meetings that pop up during the process normally. Once the report is finished ahead of schedule, the employees could turn that focus to all of the other tasks, completing them one at a time, and consistently turn out better work.

# Key Takeaway 3

**When someone refuses to prioritize or make decisions about what to take on versus what to refuse, other people will end up making the decision based on what they find important.**

## Analysis

McKeown twice allowed his decisions to be made for him by not examining those choices carefully. He started law school because so many people recommended it to him, not because he had any interest in the law. Then, when his wife had just delivered their first child, he attended a business meeting because he could not muster the courage to refuse the request. Being passive about priorities, and the choices they dictate, results in other people's priorities becoming the basis for decisions.

As a result of recent scientific developments, the common understanding of what influences decisions includes input from the people around the decisionmaker and stimuli from unexpected places. In restaurants, what someone orders might be influenced by the decor, the tempo of the music, the color of the walls, the pictures in the menu, the text in the menu's descriptions, and what other people at the table order. Businesses use their improved understanding of these stimuli to market their products, but individuals should realize that stimuli play on decisions much larger than what they decide to buy. Someone might attend medical school because their parents said that would be the choice they prefer, even if that person has no interest in medicine and does not have the skills to deal with patients. Once that person becomes a doctor, they will be in an unfulfilling job at which they have no talent. On a smaller scale, by refusing to choose the priorities that are important enough to take up the majority of available time, a person may find that they accept all other requests and must devote less and less time to their own priorities to help others pursue theirs.

# Key Takeaway 4

**Discerning what is important requires understanding that less can be better. An easy way to decide what is important enough is to immediately rule out anything that is not obviously vital to the primary goal.**

## Analysis

The guiding phrase for the Essentialist is less but better. Identifying the vital few can be a difficult process, considering how long most people have been listening to more is better advice. However, pruning out what is nonessential can result in a more focused and efficient operation. Deciding what those priorities should be can be difficult if the goal is to simply decide what is nonessential enough to cut. Instead, individuals should decide what is essential enough to keep and cut anything that is obviously nonessential or somewhere between essential and nonessential.

An example of this shift in perspective might be the case of a female corporate executive who has a long list of priorities. She may find that in the process of accomplishing her work, she has allowed her family obligations to be neglected. Meanwhile, the quality of her work has fallen as she tries to be involved in as many projects as possible. She might be afraid to say no to new opportunities because she wants to earn the trust of her employees and be accountable to the board members when they ask about the status of various projects. To that end, she has become entangled in numerous low level projects that would work just as well without her involvement. She decides to cut these first. However, beyond that point she has a difficult time deciding what is essential versus nonessential. She might feel that, while her family and her obligations to her immediate subordinates are obvious priorities, her other responsibilities in monitoring projects in progress, tending to customer relations, and advocating for the business to the public are less essential but still cannot simply be abandoned. Through the Essentialist approach, she decides that she must drop all of these non-obvious tasks, but before doing so she delegates them to new public relations and project management employees.

# Key Takeaway 5

**Focusing on the important few priorities can require an individual or organization to abandon other goals that are not vital but would be nice to have, which preserves resources and energy for the essential tasks.**

## Analysis

Trade-offs allow a business or person to consciously decide not to pursue a particular goal that would be nice to achieve, but is not necessary, in order to focus all resources on the priority goal. Southwest Airlines epitomized this in its point-to-point service. It cut out all the nonessentials in its pursuit of higher returns on investment. Other airlines that tried to copy Southwest's success struggled because they simply expanded their services.

Someone might unintentionally make trade-offs as a Nonessentialist by deciding not to attend their child's school event, instead attending a meeting that could have been skipped because of an inability to say no. Corporations, similarly, can make difficult trade-offs that do not focus on priorities when they go through bankruptcy rather than consistently making the effort to streamline operations for profitability. These are usually not conscious decisions and they are regrettable. On the other hand, a conscious trade-off would prevent the need for someone to miss a child's important school event because they would have already told the employer that certain days are off-limits for work obligations. The business might have avoided bankruptcy by making the trade-off early on to avoid accumulating too much debt, limiting growth but also ensuring that short-term debt obligations can always be met. These trade-offs may not be popular, since defining the sacrifice of growth for solvency would make the company unappealing to investors and relegate it to a smaller percentage of the market. However, they are vital for sustainable success.

# Key Takeaway 6

**Keeping the mind sharp and focused can be facilitated by intentionally isolating from distractions.**

## Analysis

Avoiding new obligations may be so difficult that the only way to focus is to completely cut off from email or phone. McKeown described his isolation while he wrote his book as "Monk Mode." That focus is aided by adequate sleep that protects the mind from the effects of sleep deprivation and encourages better problem solving because of the mental connections made during a complete sleep cycle. Also, ensuring that play will have a place in the schedule benefits creativity and relieves stress.

The benefits of isolation for focus are well documented and they are at the core of popular writers' and artists' retreats. The practice of isolating to finish an artistic work is so well recognized that an artist renting a cabin in the wilderness to finish a work is a trope in mystery, horror, and romance stories. In theory, someone so far removed from the modern distractions of telephones, email, and television would have little else to do than reflect and work. Practicing this to a lesser extreme might involve someone setting a voicemail or email away message one day each week to say that they are unavailable to focus on working without distractions, then unplugging the internet and turning off the phone until the next day. At the same time, sleep and play should be among the priorities that allow those isolated days to be productive. Sleep free of interruptions might necessitate another period of unplugged internet and turned off phone, and focused play should similarly be without the potential for interruptions. Just the possibility that an email or phone call will interrupt that designated play time can reduce its stress-relief effects.

# Key Takeaway 7

**Learning to refuse opportunities can be challenging if someone is worried about the ramifications of that refusal. They can offer to consider it after something else is accomplished or ask the requester to decide what to de-prioritize.**

## Analysis

Some people do not have the liberty to turn down any request they receive. They might feel pressured to say yes to avoid tension with coworkers or poor impressions on the boss. However, many people can say no to certain opportunities because the potential ramifications are temporary, whereas the benefits will be long term. For people who cannot say no outright, they can find less direct ways of communicating their desire to focus on a priority, such as telling the requester when a better time to schedule the obligation would be and asking them to decide what should be taken off the priority list to accommodate this new task.

For example, if a manager learned from a superior that he will be expected to come to work on Saturday to make sure that a project is completed on time, he may want to refuse that request because Saturdays he spends with his children. If he knows the supervisor to be flexible and understanding about family accommodations, he might simply respond by saying he has plans with his kids. He could also relieve the tension, if there is any, by making a joke. If, on the other hand, the supervisor is notoriously unmoved by requests for the sake of family time, the manager can refuse with an appeal to the business in regards to the necessity of keeping Saturdays free of work. The supervisor might be swayed by the argument that workers coming in on Saturday would not be focused on their tasks, trying to finish as quickly as possible without doing their best work because they want to go home. Another strategy might be to explain that the task could just as easily be accomplished by dedicating time to it in the week leading up to that Saturday, or by skipping a superfluous Monday meeting to do it the next week. None of these responses would have to sound like a no, but instead like helpful suggestions.

# Key Takeaway 8

**An individual or organization should be able to define the key goal clearly enough to know when it has been accomplished and to know how much needs to be done to reach it.**

## Analysis

Organizations tend to define their goals and mission statements in vague terms that do not define a clear goal. These statements also define multiple priorities or multiple groups to please, such as being accountable to customers, shareholders, and employees at the same time. Individuals' goals can be similarly unclear. In these cases, no one could define when those goals are accomplished.

One example of this is Google's motto, "Don't be evil." Given the range of Google's services and the many different perspectives on whether the company's operations are moral, such as regarding its censored services in China and its application of user data in advertising, whether Google has met that goal is practically impossible to determine. Even if Google's operations are deemed immoral, judging them to be evil would require defining whether evil is an ideological concept or simply another word for immoral, and then deciding what the threshold for evil behavior is.

For individuals, certain priorities may not appear to lend themselves to objective based goals. If family is someone's top priority, that is not a goal that can be accomplished. However, defining a required amount of time to spend with family members, committing to attending every one of a child's soccer games, or specifying how many times each month to call mom and dad can make the priority one that can be measured on a regular basis to check whether the family is actually getting enough attention and time in proportion with its importance.

# Key Takeaway 9

**Editing the nonessential out of all aspects of life allows the essential to become clear. Other strategies for placing emphasis on the essential include setting boundaries on when to be available for work and learning to let go of losses in projects.**

## Analysis

To achieve essentialism in a practical way, a person should apply the practices of the best editors to their lives and learn to recognize when removing one thing, like a task or a step in a process, actually benefits the overall goal. Similarly, when someone sets boundaries, such as strictly defining business hours, both the work hours and the family hours become more fulfilling. Limits such as these actually remove other, unnecessary mental blocks and distractions. Another potential mental block exists when someone resists giving up a goal because they have already devoted time or money to it. An Essentialist learns to see this sunk cost as a loss that need not be recouped.

In an example of a business owner seeking to apply essentialist principles to her business, she might first think about where editing would be most necessary to her success. She could remove a service that is taking up a higher percentage of resources without providing a comparable percentage of returns. She might also decide to reduce the number of vehicles the business owns, encouraging employees to make more efficient use of a vehicle they must share. The business owner could define her personal limits by delegating more of her responsibilities to her employees, letting them come up with solutions to problems and run their divisions without needing to check with her. This decision would let the business owner focus exclusively on her priorities during work hours and feel confident that her employees know their responsibilities. She could establish a policy that no one needs to come to work on weekends and that managers cannot pressure employees to come in outside of work hours, cutting down on the amount of time employees spend negotiating their schedules to ensure they can meet family obligations. As a result, employees could be more focused during work hours and know they need to make use of their weekdays because company email accounts will be inaccessible over the weekend. Then, the business owner could let go of unsuccessful marketing campaigns and products instead of continuing to spend money on them without seeing results.

# Key Takeaway 10

**When finding ways to eliminate the nonessential from a process, focus on creating buffers for time and resources to avoid a rush, eliminating bottlenecks rather than creating additional processes, and structuring the process as a series of small steps.**

## Analysis

Buffers are additional allowances for time and resources that ensure that unseen obstacles can be accounted for while still meeting deadline and budget expectations. Making a process more productive could involve finding an existing obstacle that limits its productivity, like a production bottleneck that is causing a backlog of work at a specific point and alleviating it. It might also help to think of the process as involving many small tasks, each requiring a little effort, than to think of it as one large task requiring a high level of effort.

In chemistry, this concept is defined as a limiting reagent. The limiting reagent is the component of a reaction that defines the volume of the result. In non-chemical terms, if a chocolate chip cookie recipe calls for one bag of chocolate chips per batch of cookies, no matter how much butter, flour, or sugar is available, the baker can only make two batches if they only have two bags of chips. A limiter might not be something as obvious as a bottleneck in a process where there is a backlog of work. Instead, it might be the fact that buying 100 bags containing six hot dogs each and 100 bags containing eight hot dog buns each for a restaurant will result in 600 hot dogs to the 800 hot dog buns, limiting the number of hot dogs sold to 600 total.

Along the same lines, creating a buffer by ensuring that the sellers always have more than enough buns and hot dogs and defining the hot dog sales process by its individual steps, starting with getting a potential buyer's attention and ending in the sale, can reduce friction in the selling process and identify more potential sticking points without adding costly initiatives and changes.

# Key Takeaway 11

**Implementing essentialism in everyday life requires that essentialism be at the center of every decision made rather than being applied only to certain decisions.**

## Analysis

Implementing essentialism in everyday life can happen by establishing routines that make the essential things the focus of every day while minimizing distractions. Presence in the current moment can also ensure that those decisions are noticed, carefully considered, and decided based on priorities.

In these tools for implementing essentialism, the practice shares many similarities with minimalist ideologies like Zen Buddhism, a connection that is particularly obvious in the importance of being present in the now but less obvious in the establishment of routines. However, Zen Buddhist monks live rigidly structured lives. They often begin their mornings early, with prayer, then work in the monastery gardens together, and eat breakfast together. Their schedules, meals, and responsibilities seldom change. Most significant is the long periods of time Japanese Zen Buddhist monks spend sitting zazen, or meditation, always at a scheduled time and all together. No monk could excuse themself because of a distraction, since the point of zazen is to eliminate distractions and focus on the teachings of the Buddha. Applying essentialism to everyday life need not be as rigid as the practices of Buddhist monks, but consistency is just as important in certain respects. An Essentialist would not skip an activity meant to eliminate distractions because of a distraction.

# Key Takeaway 12

**Leaders have the ability to enforce essentialism in their teams by choosing only the best members, clearly defining a limited range of goals and roles, optimizing communication, and following up often.**

## Analysis

A leader of a team founded on essentialist principles must first define the team's goal as narrowly as possible. This allows the leader to decide what the team members will need to do, and therefore what kinds of team members they should choose. Then, the leader would select only those members who are perfect for the roles and not pick anyone who would be redundant in the team. The leader would then communicate only what is necessary at the most necessary times, cutting out all unnecessary chatter, with the exception of checking in on the members' progress regularly to ensure that each member is getting the resources they need.

This leadership style may seem too hands-off to work, at first. After all, limiting communication from the leader would appear to allow the team members too much room for interpreting that communication without verifying with the leader that they are on the right track. The leader must trust that the members know when to ask questions and when to practice their individual problem-solving skills. This leads back to picking members who understand their roles. A leader need not decide against someone who would need more guidance. Instead, the leader could outline from the start for the team member how much guidance they expect to give, and make sure the door is always open for questions. Clearly defining member roles also allows them to understand when they will need to communicate with each other, whether they will need to solve problems for each other, and whether they should expect to check up on each other's progress. The group is therefore able to direct itself without constant involvement from the leader.

# Author's Style

Greg McKeown's style in *Essentialism* is conversational and personal. His advice is addressed directly to the reader and features many examples, anecdotes, and references. A majority of those anecdotes come from McKeown's own life, from his early childhood to the process of writing the book itself, including organizing his time to get it written and published.

Other anecdotes come from McKeown's clients, his own research, books he references, or historical tales from people such as Rosa Parks and Siddhartha Gautama. In some cases, names are left out or changed. McKeown references many other recent books on business management, goal achievement, and human behavior.

Chapters are often broken into an introductory anecdote, a description of the principle to be addressed in the chapter, an examination of its meaning and evidence to support it, and more specific advice for implementing that strategy in the reader's life. The text is occasionally broken up with large, text-based minimalist graphics featuring quotes from the book. Each chapter also has a table comparing the characteristics of an Essentialist with those of a Nonessentialist.

The advice is evenly distributed between ways to apply essentialist principles to organizations and how to apply them to individuals. It is targeted toward business readers seeking to organize their careers and, while the principles may be applicable to individuals looking to adjust priorities, such as stay-at-home parents or other unconventionally employed people, they are not addressed in the book. The examples also particularly highlight how the principles apply to executives and managers, who can set their own schedules, rearrange priorities, and refuse opportunities. There are fewer examples that provide lower level employees with models for being Essentialists at work. Advice to organizations applies equally to for profit groups as to non-profit groups. There is no business specific jargon used.

# Author's Perspective

Greg McKeown grew up in England, earned a bachelor's degree at Brigham Young University and his MBA from Stanford University's Graduate School of Business. He began working at a coaching company in college. He also worked for retained executive search firm Heidrick & Struggles International, Inc., before founding his own leadership and strategy design firm, THIS, Inc., in 2011. He co-wrote *Multipliers: How the Best Leaders Make Everyone Smarter* with Liz Wiseman in 2010. He was inducted into the World Economic Forum's Forum of Young Global Leaders in 2012, and he blogs for *Harvard Business Review* and *LinkedIn*. McKeown is now a United States citizen delivering speeches and consulting with clients all over the world. His personal experiences in his jet-set lifestyle influence the way he teaches businesses to adopt essentialist practices.

## ~~~~ END OF INSTAREAD ~~~~

Thank you for purchasing this Instaread book

**Download the Instaread mobile app to get
unlimited text & audio summaries
of bestselling books.**

# Visit Instaread.co
# to learn more.

CPSIA information can be obtained
at www.ICGtesting.com
Printed in the USA
BVHW071916120320
574764BV00006B/509

9 781945 048951